Easy Brain Exercises for Adults

100 Puzzles, Memory Games,

Math Riddles, and Other Activities

on Landscapes and Travels

This book belongs to

_____

Disclaimer

Although the author and publisher have made every effort to ensure that the information in this book was correct at press time, the author and publisher do not assume and hereby disclaim any liability to any party for any loss, damage, or disruption caused by errors or omissions, whether such errors or omissions result from negligence, accident, or any other cause.

D1335842

Table of contents

Welcome to the
EASY BRAIN EXERCISES FOR ADULTS!

On the following pages, you can find 100 easy exercises that will help keep your brain sharp! The book's theme – **Landscapes and Travels** – is sure to give you many hours of fun!

Each chapter includes activities such as:	
Begins With,	Coloring Page,
Rhyme Game,	Spot the Differences,
Unscrambling,	Math Game,
Word Search,	Math Riddle,
Maze,	Sudoku.

In case you need some help, you will find answers at the end of the book!

Good Luck!

Chapter 1

Activity 1. Begins With

For each letter listed below, write down one word associated with beaches. They can be nouns, verbs, or adjectives.

A word that begins with B is _____

A word that begins with C is _____

A word that begins with F is _____

A word that begins with I is _____

A word that begins with L is _____

A word that begins with S is _____

A word that begins with T is _____

A word that begins with U is _____

Now it's time to build and write down a meaningful sentence, including at least five of the words you wrote above.

_____

_____

_____

Beach

Activity 2. Rhyme Game

Write down two words you came up with in the previous activity; one that sounds the most positive and one the most negative. Then, find two rhyming words for each of them.

The most positive word I wrote down is _____

It rhymes with _____ and _____

The most negative word I wrote down is _____

It rhymes with _____ and _____

Activity 3. Unscrambling

Unscramble words related to beaches. They can be either nouns, verbs, or adjectives. If you have difficulty with any of them, you can find all the solutions in another activity on the next page.

ABCEH - B _ _ _ _

ALLHBCABE - B _ _ _ H _ _ _ L

NBIIIK - B _ _ _ _ I

LFCFI - C _ _ _ _

TCSOA - C _ _ _ _

LRAOC - C _ _ _ _

NDIGVI - D _ _ _ _ G

SAINDL - I _ _ _ _ D

LYSEHFILJ - J _ _ _ Y _ _ _ H

NLOGAO - L _ _ _ _ N

IFGDUREAL - L _ _ _ G _ _ _ D

ESGLAUL - S _ _ _ _ _ _ L

AELSLEHS - S _ _ S _ _ _ L

YSNUN - S _ _ _ _

TNNSUA - S _ _ _ _ N

AROBRSUFD - S _ _ _ B _ _ _ D

NIWSMGMI - S _ _ _ _ _ _ G

KNSURT - T _ _ _ _ S

SWVEA - W _ _ _ _

TAYCH - Y _ _ _ _

Activity 4. Word Search

Find and mark on the grid words, which are listed below. You can spot them horizontally or vertically – backwards and forwards.

BEACH	CORAL	LIFEGUARD	SURFBOARD
BEACHBALL	DIVING	SEAGULL	SWIMMING
BIKINI	ISLAND	SEASHELL	TRUNKS
CLIFF	JELLYFISH	SUNNY	WAVES
COAST	LAGOON	SUNTAN	YACHT

```
D  Y  B  S  U  N  N  Y  R  G  N  I  V  I  D
A  B  E  A  C  H  S  Y  Q  F  K  B  W  I  P
J  O  A  G  U  B  W  G  V  F  M  B  A  Z  K
L  H  C  B  D  R  I  Z  O  I  V  W  V  Q  S
L  H  H  W  M  Z  M  H  M  L  W  F  E  M  K
U  S  B  P  E  U  M  S  H  C  C  A  S  S  N
G  E  A  K  E  O  I  I  E  D  O  M  D  U  U
A  A  L  A  V  C  N  F  Y  N  A  X  I  N  R
E  S  L  V  L  T  G  Y  P  E  S  R  D  T  T
S  H  P  K  V  N  I  L  S  N  T  E  A  A  I
Y  E  C  N  W  I  S  L  A  N  D  U  Y  N  C
A  L  O  P  Z  P  L  E  I  N  O  O  G  A  L
C  L  R  X  Z  D  R  J  X  I  N  I  K  I  B
H  Z  A  T  L  I  F  E  G  U  A  R  D  Y  A
T  A  L  Y  Q  H  S  U  R  F  B  O  A  R  D
```

Answers on page 84

Beach

Activity 5. Maze

Find the way out going through the maze.

Activity 6. Coloring Page

Use your imagination and color the picture.

Activity 7. Spot the Differences

Find five differences in the second picture.

Activity 8. Math Game

The thick frame has a 3x3 grid with places for nine numbers. The squares outside of it are sums of the digits in the grid's columns, rows, and diagonals – follow the arrows.

Fill in all the blanks with whole numbers. Note that they may sometimes repeat.

Activity 9. Math Riddle

Solve the equation, knowing that each identical picture is assigned a specific number. If possible, try not to take any notes.

$$\text{★} \times \text{★} = 25$$

$$\text{⛵} + \text{★} = 7$$

$$\text{🦄} - \text{⛵} = 4$$

$$\text{🦄} - \text{★} + \text{⛵} = \ldots$$

Answers on page 85

Activity 10. Sudoku

There are 81 squares in a 9x9 grid in front of you. Some of them already contain numbers, and your task is to fill in the rest.

To complete it correctly, ensure that each of the nine 3x3 grids, columns, and rows contains all the digits from 1 to 9.

9		1	6		5			3
	7	3	4					6
2	5				7	1		9
	8	4	9		2			
3	9	2		7	6		1	8
	6				8			2
	3			9	1	5		4
4		8	7					1
	1			6			2	7

Congratulations!

You have just finished the first chapter of this book!

Chapter 2

Activity 1. Begins With

For each letter listed below, write down one word associated with safaris. They can be nouns, verbs, or adjectives.

A word that begins with A is _____

A word that begins with E is _____

A word that begins with G is _____

A word that begins with H is _____

A word that begins with M is _____

A word that begins with S is _____

A word that begins with T is _____

A word that begins with W is _____

Now it's time to build and write down a meaningful sentence, including at least five of the words you wrote above.

_____

_____

_____

Safari

Activity 2. Rhyme Game

Write down two words you came up with in the previous activity; one that sounds the most positive and one the most negative. Then, find two rhyming words for each of them.

The most positive word I wrote down is _____

It rhymes with _____ and _____

The most negative word I wrote down is _____

It rhymes with _____ and _____

Activity 3. Unscrambling

Unscramble words related to safaris. They can be either nouns, verbs, or adjectives. If you have difficulty with any of them, you can find all the solutions in another activity on the next page.

CAAICA - A _ _ _ _ _

IRAAFC - A _ _ _ _ _

ABBBOA - B _ _ _ _ _

BOFAFUL - B _ _ _ _ _ O

HECTEHA - C _ _ _ _ _ H

ACBOR - C _ _ _ _

PEEALHTN - E _ _ _ _ _ _ T

ZAELLGE - G _ _ _ _ _ E

IAGFREF - G _ _ _ _ _ E

RLNGDASAS - G _ _ _ S _ _ _ D

PHIOP - H _ _ _ _

NYAEH - H _ _ _ _

OSNISEL - L _ _ _ _ _ S

IONATRGMI - M _ _ _ A _ _ _ N

NIRHO - R _ _ _ _

NAAVSNA - S _ _ _ _ _ A

HSUSRB - S _ _ _ _ _

CTPIOALR - T _ _ _ I _ _ L

AHORTWG - W _ _ _ _ _ G

BERZA - Z _ _ _ _

Chapter 2

Activity 4. Word Search

Find and mark on the grid words, which are listed below. You can spot them horizontally or vertically – backwards and forwards.

ACACIA	COBRA	HIPPO	SAVANNA
AFRICA	ELEPHANT	HYENA	SHRUBS
BAOBAB	GAZELLE	LIONESS	TROPICAL
BUFFALO	GIRAFFE	MIGRATION	WARTHOG
CHEETAH	GRASSLAND	RHINO	ZEBRA

```
D  D  V  B  L  I  G  K  A  F  R  I  C  A  W
A  N  Q  N  F  X  I  H  M  Q  I  M  Y  O  A
C  A  U  G  W  I  R  Y  Z  A  R  B  E  Z  R
A  L  T  Y  C  A  A  E  T  O  A  M  F  W  T
C  S  R  L  D  E  F  N  H  B  F  X  A  O  H
I  S  I  U  B  G  F  A  I  U  A  J  N  N  O
A  A  L  I  O  N  E  S  S  Z  S  R  N  I  G
B  R  H  G  Z  O  L  A  F  F  U  B  A  H  S
J  G  A  J  C  E  L  L  E  Z  A  G  V  R  G
Q  A  T  B  A  O  B  A  B  N  Z  G  A  F  B
W  R  E  Z  E  L  E  P  H  A  N  T  S  P  Z
F  B  E  I  T  M  N  O  I  T  A  R  G  I  M
X  O  H  A  V  F  Y  X  P  S  H  R  U  B  S
W  C  C  G  L  A  C  I  P  O  R  T  J  J  J
C  Z  Y  S  P  W  X  I  O  N  S  V  Y  O  B
```

Answers on page 86

Safari

Activity 5. Maze

Find the way out going through the maze.

Chapter 2

Activity 6. Coloring Page

Use your imagination and color the picture.

Safari

Activity 7. Spot the Differences

Find five differences in the second picture.

Activity 8. Math Game

The thick frame has a 3x3 grid with places for nine numbers. The squares outside of it are sums of the digits in the grid's columns, rows, and diagonals – follow the arrows.

Fill in all the blanks with whole numbers. Note that they may sometimes repeat.

Chapter 2

Activity 9. Math Riddle

Solve the equation, knowing that each identical picture is assigned a specific number. If possible, try not to take any notes.

$$\text{🐘} + \text{🐘} = 14$$

$$\text{🌳} - \text{🐘} = 1$$

$$\text{🌳} \div \text{👤} = 2$$

$$\text{🌳} + \text{🐘} - \text{👤} = \ldots$$

Answers on page 87

Safari

Activity 10. Sudoku

There are 81 squares in a 9x9 grid in front of you. Some of them already contain numbers, and your task is to fill in the rest.

To complete it correctly, ensure that each of the nine 3x3 grids, columns, and rows contains all the digits from 1 to 9.

				4	9		7	2
1							8	9
	7	9	5	1			4	3
2					5	4	6	8
	9		1		8			7
7	8	6			3			
4			2	9	6	8	3	1
9		1						6
		8	3		1	7	9	

Congratulations!

You have just finished the second chapter of this book!

Chapter 3

Activity 1. Begins With

For each letter listed below, write down one word associated with jungles. They can be nouns, verbs, or adjectives.

A word that begins with C is _____

A word that begins with H is _____

A word that begins with L is _____

A word that begins with N is _____

A word that begins with P is _____

A word that begins with R is _____

A word that begins with T is _____

A word that begins with W is _____

Now it's time to build and write down a meaningful sentence, including at least five of the words you wrote above.

_____

_____

_____

Jungle

Activity 2. Rhyme Game

Write down two words you came up with in the previous activity; one that sounds the most positive and one the most negative. Then, find two rhyming words for each of them.

The most positive word I wrote down is _____

It rhymes with _____ and _____

The most negative word I wrote down is _____

It rhymes with _____ and _____

Activity 3. Unscrambling

Unscramble words related to jungles. They can be either nouns, verbs, or adjectives. If you have difficulty with any of them, you can find all the solutions in another activity on the next page.

IMLLAORDA - A _ _ _ D _ _ _ O

OBOBAM - B _ _ _ _ O

FUBTYLTER - B _ _ _ E _ _ _ Y

ACYBPRAA - C _ _ Y _ _ _ A

EMANLOHEC - C _ _ _ E _ _ _ N

OARLLIG - G _ _ _ _ _ A

UDHIM - H _ _ _ _

ERLUM - L _ _ _ _

ALREPDO - L _ _ _ _ _ D

NIALA - L _ _ _ _

ENMOKY - M _ _ _ _ _

GOATRNANU - O _ _ _ G _ _ _ N

NPADA - P _ _ _ _

ORATRP - P _ _ _ _ _

AFOTIRSRNE - R _ _ _ F _ _ _ _T

OLHST - S _ _ _ _

ASEKN - S _ _ _ _

IRTEG - T _ _ _ _

NTAOCU - T _ _ _ _ N

LFEALWTRA - W _ _ _ R _ _ _ L

Chapter 3

Activity 4. Word Search

Find and mark on the grid words, which are listed below. You can spot them horizontally or vertically – backwards and forwards.

ARMADILLO	GORILLA	MONKEY	SLOTH
BAMBOO	HUMID	ORANGUTAN	SNAKE
BUTTERFLY	LEMUR	PANDA	TIGER
CAPYBARA	LEOPARD	PARROT	TOUCAN
CHAMELEON	LIANA	RAINFOREST	WATERFALL

```
S  N  A  K  E  E  R  I  F  R  W  S  P  L  A
C  J  P  A  N  D  A  U  P  O  J  V  R  O  U
Y  O  R  A  N  G  U  T  A  N  Q  F  Q  X  R
E  N  G  N  O  E  L  E  M  A  H  C  P  M  A
K  D  I  M  U  H  S  L  O  T  H  H  Z  C  I
N  N  I  T  S  U  E  A  N  A  I  L  T  B  N
O  K  J  L  E  O  P  A  R  D  M  T  O  U  F
M  I  G  A  C  Y  B  N  M  G  U  O  R  T  O
A  R  A  B  Y  P  A  C  A  O  H  U  R  T  R
L  E  M  U  R  H  M  I  E  R  G  C  A  E  E
O  L  S  P  L  H  B  X  P  I  Y  A  P  R  S
U  T  I  G  E  R  O  I  L  L  H  N  Y  F  T
J  T  I  V  S  T  O  R  I  L  X  Y  J  L  G
L  L  A  F  R  E  T  A  W  A  H  H  K  Y  K
D  W  A  R  M  A  D  I  L  L  O  P  T  B  Z
```

Answers on page 88

Jungle

Activity 5. Maze

Find the way out going through the maze.

Chapter 3

Activity 6. Coloring Page

Use your imagination and color the picture.

Jungle

Activity 7. Spot the Differences

Find five differences in the second picture.

Activity 8. Math Game

The thick frame has a 3x3 grid with places for nine numbers. The squares outside of it are sums of the digits in the grid's columns, rows, and diagonals – follow the arrows.

Fill in all the blanks with whole numbers. Note that they may sometimes repeat.

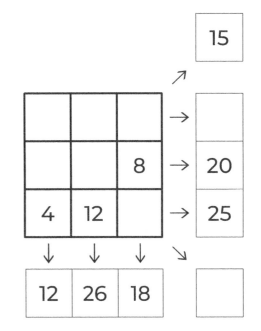

Answers on pages 88-89

Activity 9. Math Riddle

Solve the equation, knowing that each identical picture is assigned a specific number. If possible, try not to take any notes.

$$\text{(toucan)} + \text{(toucan)} + \text{(toucan)} = 12$$

$$\text{(palm tree)} - \text{(toucan)} = 2$$

$$\text{(leaf)} \times \text{(palm tree)} = 30$$

$$\text{(leaf)} + \text{(toucan)} - \text{(palm tree)} = \ldots$$

Answers on page 89

Jungle

Activity 10. Sudoku

There are 81 squares in a 9x9 grid in front of you. Some of them already contain numbers, and your task is to fill in the rest.

To complete it correctly, ensure that each of the nine 3x3 grids, columns, and rows contains all the digits from 1 to 9.

3			8	7		2		6
6		9		1		4		
2	1		4		5	8		9
1				5			2	4
	6		2					5
4	2	5			7			
8	3				1		4	2
7	9			4				
5				2		6		3

Congratulations!

You have just finished the third chapter of this book!

Chapter 4

Activity 1. Begins With

For each letter listed below, write down one word associated with forests. They can be nouns, verbs, or adjectives.

A word that begins with A is _____

A word that begins with B is _____

A word that begins with H is _____

A word that begins with M is _____

A word that begins with P is _____

A word that begins with R is _____

A word that begins with S is _____

A word that begins with W is_____

Now it's time to build and write down a meaningful sentence, including at least five of the words you wrote above.

_____

_____

_____

Forest

Activity 2. Rhyme Game

Write down two words you came up with in the previous activity; one that sounds the most positive and one the most negative. Then, find two rhyming words for each of them.

The most positive word I wrote down is _____

It rhymes with _____ and _____

The most negative word I wrote down is _____

It rhymes with _____ and _____

Activity 3. Unscrambling

Unscramble words related to forests. They can be either nouns, verbs, or adjectives. If you have difficulty with any of them, you can find all the solutions in another activity on the next page.

CARON - A _ _ _ _

REDABG - B _ _ _ _ _

OSBRA - B _ _ _ _

CARHNB - B _ _ _ _ H

MSOACSP - C _ _ _ _ _ S

GEDEOHHG - H _ _ _ E _ _ G

ESVEAL - L _ _ _ _ _

ELPMA - M _ _ _ _

TSOMUOQI - M _ _ _ U _ _O

OUMHMSOR - M _ _ _ R _ _ M

OCENPNIE - P _ _ _ C _ _ E

EGARRN - R _ _ _ _ R

ORTOS - R _ _ _ _

PUSCER - S _ _ _ _ E

ERSURIQL - S _ _ _ _ _ _ L

KTSCI - S _ _ _ _

AWMSP - S _ _ _ _

URKTN - T _ _ _ _

IWEHSLT - W _ _ _ _ _ E

DKEOWPOCER - W _ _ _ P _ _ _ _ R

Chapter 4

Activity 4. Word Search

Find and mark on the grid words, which are listed below. You can spot them horizontally or vertically – backwards and forwards.

ACORN	HEDGEHOG	PINECONE	STICK
BADGER	LEAVES	RANGER	SWAMP
BOARS	MAPLE	ROOTS	TRUNK
BRANCH	MOSQUITO	SPRUCE	WHISTLE
COMPASS	MUSHROOM	SQUIRREL	WOODPECKER

```
W  G  I  J  T  O  H  E  D  G  E  H  O  G  S
O  F  K  D  M  R  E  G  N  A  R  I  O  S  P
O  D  I  C  O  M  P  A  S  S  S  X  Z  T  R
D  X  D  K  S  A  K  L  E  A  V  E  S  I  U
P  C  U  S  Q  M  U  S  H  R  O  O  M  C  C
E  A  N  W  U  B  R  A  N  C  H  U  Q  K  E
C  H  D  A  I  A  E  U  G  L  T  Z  R  N  S
K  T  B  M  T  H  L  S  B  O  A  R  S  B  T
E  Z  Y  P  O  U  T  S  R  B  Q  P  T  B  O
R  A  P  Y  A  D  S  V  O  H  H  Q  F  N  O
E  A  L  V  Q  T  I  A  N  R  O  C  A  C  R
B  A  D  G  E  R  H  E  N  O  C  E  N  I  P
C  M  H  R  Q  F  W  X  T  R  U  N  K  K  T
S  Q  U  I  R  R  E  L  X  U  Z  T  V  C  O
J  J  C  T  M  A  P  L  E  Q  Z  Z  K  P  O
```

Answers on page 90

Activity 5. Maze

Find the way out going through the maze.

Chapter 4

Activity 6. Coloring Page

Use your imagination and color the picture.

Forest

Activity 7. Spot the Differences

Find five differences in the second picture.

Activity 8. Math Game

The thick frame has a 3x3 grid with places for nine numbers. The squares outside of it are sums of the digits in the grid's columns, rows, and diagonals – follow the arrows.

Fill in all the blanks with whole numbers. Note that they may sometimes repeat.

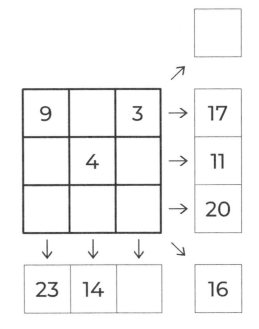

Activity 9. Math Riddle

Solve the equation, knowing that each identical picture is assigned a specific number. If possible, try not to take any notes.

$$\text{🌲} + \text{🌲} = 12$$

$$\text{🌲} \times \text{🌲} = 24$$

$$\text{🌳} - \text{🌲} = 4$$

$$\text{🌲} \times \text{🌲} \div \text{🌳} = \ldots$$

Answers on page 91

Activity 10. Sudoku

There are 81 squares in a 9x9 grid in front of you. Some of them already contain numbers, and your task is to fill in the rest.

To complete it correctly, ensure that each of the nine 3x3 grids, columns, and rows contains all the digits from 1 to 9.

4	2	6		1			8	
				2		1		
7					3			2
	7	2			5	9	4	
9			2	7		8		
6	1			8			3	7
2	6	9		4			7	
3			6		2			
1	4	8			7		2	9

Congratulations!

You have just finished the fourth chapter of this book!

Chapter 5

Activity 1. Begins With

For each letter listed below, write down one word associated with hiking. They can be nouns, verbs, or adjectives.

A word that begins with B is _____

A word that begins with E is _____

A word that begins with F is _____

A word that begins with I is _____

A word that begins with O is _____

A word that begins with R is _____

A word that begins with S is _____

A word that begins with V is _____

Now it's time to build and write down a meaningful sentence, including at least five of the words you wrote above.

_____

_____

_____

Hiking

Activity 2. Rhyme Game

Write down two words you came up with in the previous activity; one that sounds the most positive and one the most negative. Then, find two rhyming words for each of them.

The most positive word I wrote down is _____

It rhymes with _____ and _____

The most negative word I wrote down is _____

It rhymes with _____ and _____

Activity 3. Unscrambling

Unscramble words related to hiking. They can be either nouns, verbs, or adjectives. If you have difficulty with any of them, you can find all the solutions in another activity on the next page.

VDAEUENRT - A _ _ _ N _ _ _ E   EREOBSV - O _ _ _ _ _ E

ABCCKKPA - B _ _ _ _ _ _ K   OPOTH - P _ _ _ _

AEDNABG - B _ _ _ _ _ E   EPRRAEP - P _ _ _ _ _ E

MCAARE - C _ _ _ _ _   EERUSC - R _ _ _ _ _

TEOFFR - E _ _ _ _ T   ANIWHSCD - S _ _ _ _ _ _ H

TSNISEF - F _ _ _ _ _ S   LHESETR - S _ _ _ _ _ R

IUEGD - G _ _ _ _   URESNECNS - S _ _ _ C _ _ _ N

UJYINR - I _ _ _ _ _   NTIGRI - T _ _ _ _ G

IPSINRGIN - I _ _ _ I _ _ _ G   EVYLAL - V _ _ _ _ _

TMUONANI - M _ _ _ _ _ _ N   OCNLAVO - V _ _ _ _ _ O

Chapter 5

Activity 4. Word Search

Find and mark on the grid words, which are listed below. You can spot them horizontally or vertically – backwards and forwards.

ADVENTURE	FITNESS	OBSERVE	SHELTER
BACKPACK	GUIDE	PHOTO	SUNSCREEN
BANDAGE	INJURY	PREPARE	TIRING
CAMERA	INSPIRING	RESCUE	VALLEY
EFFORT	MOUNTAIN	SANDWICH	VOLCANO

```
F  T  Y  N  Z  U  N  P  O  B  S  E  R  V  E
F  X  F  K  P  H  O  T  O  G  B  Y  Q  A  Q
I  U  I  B  W  G  H  A  V  F  V  P  I  L  L
K  F  T  E  S  U  N  S  C  R  E  E  N  L  W
C  E  N  G  E  R  U  T  N  E  V  D  A  E  E
A  R  E  A  T  W  V  O  L  C  A  N  O  Y  J
P  H  S  D  I  F  H  K  C  R  E  S  C  U  E
K  M  S  N  N  M  O  U  N  T  A  I  N  B  S
C  G  I  A  S  Z  T  J  W  Q  N  G  C  N  A
A  U  N  B  P  T  I  Y  F  L  I  H  F  U  N
B  I  J  R  I  R  R  O  C  A  M  E  R  A  D
M  D  U  Z  R  O  I  E  R  A  P  E  R  P  W
J  E  R  R  I  F  N  Y  P  P  J  K  W  T  I
I  W  Y  C  N  F  G  S  H  E  L  T  E  R  C
J  Q  O  K  G  E  D  K  L  S  L  G  V  S  H
```

Answers on page 92

Hiking

Activity 5. Maze

Find the way out going through the maze.

START

FINISH

Chapter 5

Activity 6. Coloring Page

Use your imagination and color the picture.

Hiking

Activity 7. Spot the Differences

Find five differences in the second picture.

Activity 8. Math Game

The thick frame has a 3x3 grid with places for nine numbers. The squares outside of it are sums of the digits in the grid's columns, rows, and diagonals – follow the arrows.

Fill in all the blanks with whole numbers. Note that they may sometimes repeat.

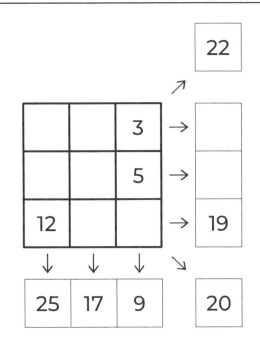

Answers on pages 92-93   - 41 -

Chapter 5

Activity 9. Math Riddle

Solve the equation, knowing that each identical picture is assigned a specific number. If possible, try not to take any notes.

$$\text{(backpack)} \times \text{(backpack)} = 49$$

$$\text{(guide)} + \text{(backpack)} = 10$$

$$\text{(compass)} \div \text{(guide)} = 3$$

$$\text{(guide)} + \text{(compass)} - \text{(backpack)} = \ldots$$

Answers on page 93

Hiking

Activity 10. Sudoku

There are 81 squares in a 9x9 grid in front of you. Some of them already contain numbers, and your task is to fill in the rest.

To complete it correctly, ensure that each of the nine 3x3 grids, columns, and rows contains all the digits from 1 to 9.

9			8		2	4		
			4	5		1		7
	6			9			8	5
3		5			4	7		6
1	9		7		5			4
4	7		3	2				8
	8						3	1
6		9	5		7	8		2
2				1	8			9

Congratulations!

You have just finished the fifth chapter of this book!

Chapter 6

Activity 1. Begins With

For each letter listed below, write down one word associated with camping. They can be nouns, verbs, or adjectives.

A word that begins with C is _____

A word that begins with F is _____

A word that begins with G is _____

A word that begins with L Is _____

A word that begins with N is _____

A word that begins with P is _____

A word that begins with S is _____

A word that begins with W is_____

Now it's time to build and write down a meaningful sentence, including at least five of the words you wrote above.

_____

_____

_____

Camping

Activity 2. Rhyme Game

Write down two words you came up with in the previous activity; one that sounds the most positive and one the most negative. Then, find two rhyming words for each of them.

The most positive word I wrote down is _____

It rhymes with _____ and _____

The most negative word I wrote down is _____

It rhymes with _____ and _____

Activity 3. Unscrambling

Unscramble words related to camping. They can be either nouns, verbs, or adjectives. If you have difficulty with any of them, you can find all the solutions in another activity on the next page.

OAUIBCNLRS - B _ _ O _ _ L _ _ S   UELRIES - L _ _ _ _ _ E

EAPMCR - C _ _ _ _ R   AHCSMET - M _ _ _ _ _ S

ACEFPIMR - C _ _ _ _ _ _ E   TINOHMOLG - M _ _ _ L _ _ _ T

ENMPUEQIT - E _ _ _ P _ _ _ T   RENTUA - N _ _ _ _ E

SIIFHGN - F _ _ _ _ _ G   TOUSOROD - O _ _ D _ _ _ S

TIRGUA - G _ _ _ _ R   NDAGLIDP - P _ _ _ L _ _ G

AOCMMHK - H _ _ _ _ _ K   LETNPELRE - R _ _ _ L _ _ _ T

TCSNIE - I _ _ _ _ _   REYNECS - S _ _ _ _ _ Y

AYKKA - K _ _ _ _   KSCAN - S _ _ _ _

NRTANEL - L _ _ _ _ _ N   FLIELIDW - W _ _ D _ _ _ E

Chapter 6

Activity 4. Word Search

Find and mark on the grid words, which are listed below. You can spot them horizontally or vertically – backwards and forwards.

BINOCULARS	GUITAR	LEISURE	PADDLING
CAMPER	HAMMOCK	MATCHES	REPELLENT
CAMPFIRE	INSECT	MOONLIGHT	SCENERY
EQUIPMENT	KAYAK	NATURE	SNACK
FISHING	LANTERN	OUTDOORS	WILDLIFE

```
Q  M  T  M  A  T  C  H  E  S  G  B  G  P  S
E  O  B  F  C  A  A  G  U  W  I  N  L  K  C
Q  O  X  I  M  W  I  Y  S  M  N  R  E  A  E
U  N  T  S  Q  R  X  I  M  D  S  Y  I  Y  N
I  L  E  H  E  R  U  T  A  N  E  M  S  A  E
P  I  R  I  B  H  A  M  M  O  C  K  U  K  R
M  G  I  N  M  X  F  J  T  Q  T  J  R  G  Y
E  H  F  G  P  A  D  D  L  I  N  G  E  U  Q
N  T  P  N  R  E  T  N  A  L  J  P  T  I  V
T  S  M  E  R  E  P  E  L  L  E  N  T  T  P
S  R  A  L  U  C  O  N  I  B  C  B  B  A  I
S  O  C  U  E  G  C  A  M  P  E  R  P  R  E
G  V  K  S  N  A  C  K  R  Z  Q  J  F  I  L
Q  G  F  C  O  U  T  D  O  O  R  S  Z  O  Q
J  O  K  W  I  L  D  L  I  F  E  J  H  M  Z
```

Answers on page 94

Activity 5. Maze

Find the way out going through the maze.

Chapter 6

Activity 6. Coloring Page

Use your imagination and color the picture.

Camping

Activity 7. Spot the Differences

Find five differences in the second picture.

Activity 8. Math Game

The thick frame has a 3x3 grid with places for nine numbers. The squares outside of it are sums of the digits in the grid's columns, rows, and diagonals – follow the arrows.

Fill in all the blanks with whole numbers. Note that they may sometimes repeat.

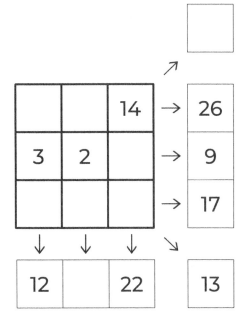

Answers on pages 94-95

Chapter 6

Activity 9. Math Riddle

Solve the equation, knowing that each identical picture is assigned a specific number. If possible, try not to take any notes.

$$\text{🔥} + \text{🔥} + \text{🔥} = 18$$

$$\text{🎣} \times \text{🔥} = 24$$

$$\text{🔪} - \text{🎣} = 3$$

$$\text{🔪} + \text{🎣} + \text{🔥} = \ldots$$

Answers on page 95

Camping

Activity 10. Sudoku

There are 81 squares in a 9x9 grid in front of you. Some of them already contain numbers, and your task is to fill in the rest.

To complete it correctly, ensure that each of the nine 3x3 grids, columns, and rows contains all the digits from 1 to 9.

1		5	6	2		8	3	
	4	8	1	7	3	5		6
6	3		5	8			1	7
5	2		8					
	8	7						
		4	3		5		8	
			9	1		4	5	
	5		7		8			9
		2	4	5		1		

Congratulations!

You have just finished the sixth chapter of this book!

Chapter 7

Activity 1. Begins With

For each letter listed below, write down one word associated with the countryside. They can be nouns, verbs, or adjectives.

A word that begins with C is _____

A word that begins with F is _____

A word that begins with G is _____

A word that begins with H is _____

A word that begins with O is _____

A word that begins with P is _____

A word that begins with S is _____

A word that begins with W is _____

Now it's time to build and write down a meaningful sentence, including at least five of the words you wrote above.

_____

_____

_____

Countryside

Activity 2. Rhyme Game

Write down two words you came up with in the previous activity; one that sounds the most positive and one the most negative. Then, find two rhyming words for each of them.

The most positive word I wrote down is _____

It rhymes with _____ and _____

The most negative word I wrote down is _____

It rhymes with _____ and _____

Activity 3. Unscrambling

Unscramble words related to the countryside. They can be either nouns, verbs, or adjectives. If you have difficulty with any of them, you can find all the solutions in another activity on the next page.

RHUIBDSOE - B _ _ _ H _ _ _ E   EMOADW - M _ _ _ _ W

KHCEINC - C _ _ _ _ _ N   CORHDAR - O _ _ _ _ _ D

RFMRAE - F _ _ _ _ _   SEAUPRT - P _ _ _ _ _ E

AOSFEUHRM - F _ _ _ H _ _ _ E   OERCDPU - P _ _ _ _ _ E

NFEEC - F _ _ _ _   ROCEASCRW - S _ _ _ E _ _ _ W

ELFID - F _ _ _ _   EHSEP - S _ _ _ _

SRSAG - G _ _ _ _   FSLUREONW - S _ _ _ L _ _ _ R

RAEHVTS - H _ _ _ _ _ T   ATCRTOR - T _ _ _ _ _ R

SEEHUOHN - H _ _ _ O _ _ E   AHTEW - W _ _ _ _

SOERH - H _ _ _ _   NMWLLIDI - W _ _ _ _ _ _ L

Chapter 7

Activity 4. Word Search

Find and mark on the grid words, which are listed below. You can spot them horizontally or vertically – backwards and forwards.

BIRDHOUSE	FIELD	MEADOW	SHEEP
CHICKEN	GRASS	ORCHARD	SUNFLOWER
FARMER	HARVEST	PASTURE	TRACTOR
FARMHOUSE	HENHOUSE	PRODUCE	WHEAT
FENCE	HORSE	SCARECROW	WINDMILL

```
W  K  F  O  T  R  A  C  T  O  R  B  M  C  D
I  T  D  K  T  L  A  P  Q  E  S  R  O  H  J
N  B  P  R  W  G  R  E  M  R  A  F  T  I  P
D  I  E  H  O  P  H  J  G  K  H  P  N  C  A
M  R  E  S  R  O  E  F  R  Z  H  H  A  K  S
I  D  H  U  C  S  N  E  A  G  V  A  M  E  T
L  H  S  N  E  A  H  N  S  E  P  R  F  N  U
L  O  A  F  R  E  O  C  S  K  N  V  Q  Z  R
P  U  N  L  A  W  U  E  E  F  I  E  L  D  E
R  S  T  O  C  H  S  Z  I  D  M  S  T  A  S
O  E  B  W  S  E  E  D  V  U  W  T  L  U  T
D  J  X  E  F  A  T  S  M  E  A  D  O  W  K
U  Y  W  R  D  T  R  G  W  H  W  D  O  U  R
C  E  S  U  O  H  M  R  A  F  J  K  X  N  F
E  Y  X  P  N  Q  R  D  R  A  H  C  R  O  X
```

Answers on page 96

Countryside

Activity 5. Maze

Find the way out going through the maze.

START

FINISH

Chapter 7

Activity 6. Coloring Page

Use your imagination and color the picture.

Activity 7. Spot the Differences

Find five differences in the second picture.

Activity 8. Math Game

The thick frame has a 3x3 grid with places for nine numbers. The squares outside of it are sums of the digits in the grid's columns, rows, and diagonals – follow the arrows.

Fill in all the blanks with whole numbers. Note that they may sometimes repeat.

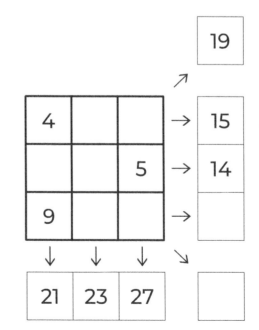

Chapter 7

Activity 9. Math Riddle

Solve the equation, knowing that each identical picture is assigned a specific number. If possible, try not to take any notes.

$$\text{(watering can)} \times \text{(watering can)} = 9$$

$$\text{(windmill)} + \text{(watering can)} = 7$$

$$\text{(dairy)} \div \text{(windmill)} = 2$$

$$\text{(windmill)} + \text{(dairy)} - \text{(watering can)} = \ldots$$

   Answers on page 97

Countryside

Activity 10. Sudoku

There are 81 squares in a 9x9 grid in front of you. Some of them already contain numbers, and your task is to fill in the rest.

To complete it correctly, ensure that each of the nine 3x3 grids, columns, and rows contains all the digits from 1 to 9.

1	8			7		6	2	
	6	5		9		7		1
			1		6	9		8
	9	7					8	
4			2	8		3		7
8		2			7	5	1	
9		6	4	2	1			3
				3				
	1	3	9			8	2	

Congratulations!

You have just finished the seventh chapter of this book!

Chapter 8

Activity 1. Begins With

For each letter listed below, write down one word associated with a city. They can be nouns, verbs, or adjectives.

A word that begins with B is _____

A word that begins with D is _____

A word that begins with F is _____

A word that begins with L is _____

A word that begins with N is _____

A word that begins with S is _____

A word that begins with V is _____

A word that begins with W is _____

Now it's time to build and write down a meaningful sentence, including at least five of the words you wrote above.

_____

_____

_____

City

Activity 2. Rhyme Game

Write down two words you came up with in the previous activity; one that sounds the most positive and one the most negative. Then, find two rhyming words for each of them.

The most positive word I wrote down is _____

It rhymes with _____ and _____

The most negative word I wrote down is _____

It rhymes with _____ and _____

Activity 3. Unscrambling

Unscramble words related to a city. They can be either nouns, verbs, or adjectives. If you have difficulty with any of them, you can find all the solutions in another activity on the next page.

GDRBEI - B _ _ _ _ E

UCRHHC - C _ _ _ _ H

NOECCTR - C _ _ _ _ _ T

FNOUINAT - F _ _ _ _ _ _ N

YARMO - M _ _ _ _

EMUMNNTO - M _ _ _ M _ _ T

SUMUEM - M _ _ _ _ _

CPAELA - P _ _ _ E

APTRESDENI - P _ _ _ S _ _ _ _ N

VIERR - R _ _ _ _

EGTHISSGNIE - S _ _ H _ _ E _ _ _ G

PKRCYRASSE - S _ _ S _ _ A _ _ R

OVURINSE - S _ _ _ E _ _R

MSUTIAD - S _ _ _ _ _ M

OSAINTT - S _ _ _ _ _ N

LMTEPE - T _ _ _ _ E

OTRUITS - T _ _ _ _ _ T

WOETR - T _ _ _ _

NTISVYUIER - U _ _ V _ _ S _ _ Y

WEATRKPAR - W _ _ _ R _ _ _ K

Chapter 8

Activity 4. Word Search

Find and mark on the grid words, which are listed below. You can spot them horizontally or vertically – backwards and forwards.

BRIDGE	MONUMENT	SIGHTSEEING	TEMPLE
CHURCH	MUSEUM	SKYSCRAPER	TOURIST
CONCERT	PALACE	SOUVENIR	TOWER
FOUNTAIN	PEDESTRIAN	STADIUM	UNIVERSITY
MAYOR	RIVER	STATION	WATERPARK

```
F  S  J  M  S  O  U  V  E  N  I  R  U  S  B
F  A  G  D  Z  M  O  N  U  M  E  N  T  W  S
R  W  N  Y  T  I  S  R  E  V  I  N  U  P  S
E  A  I  E  P  F  C  M  U  S  E  U  M  E  Y
P  T  E  M  P  L  E  O  B  M  T  S  Q  D  R
A  E  E  P  A  L  A  C  E  B  R  T  P  E  N
R  R  S  Z  R  S  L  U  T  X  E  A  P  S  I
C  P  T  W  M  Z  C  P  O  A  C  D  J  T  A
S  A  H  E  A  X  Z  N  W  C  N  I  S  R  T
Y  R  G  G  Y  A  F  I  E  T  O  U  T  I  N
K  K  I  D  O  E  E  D  R  Q  C  M  A  A  U
S  N  S  I  R  Y  R  I  V  E  R  X  T  N  O
E  R  L  R  C  H  U  R  C  H  S  E  I  Z  F
K  C  Q  B  V  G  W  S  K  W  M  F  O  B  S
W  D  T  O  U  R  I  S  T  D  P  N  N  Y  E
```

Answers on page 98

Activity 5. Maze

Find the way out going through the maze.

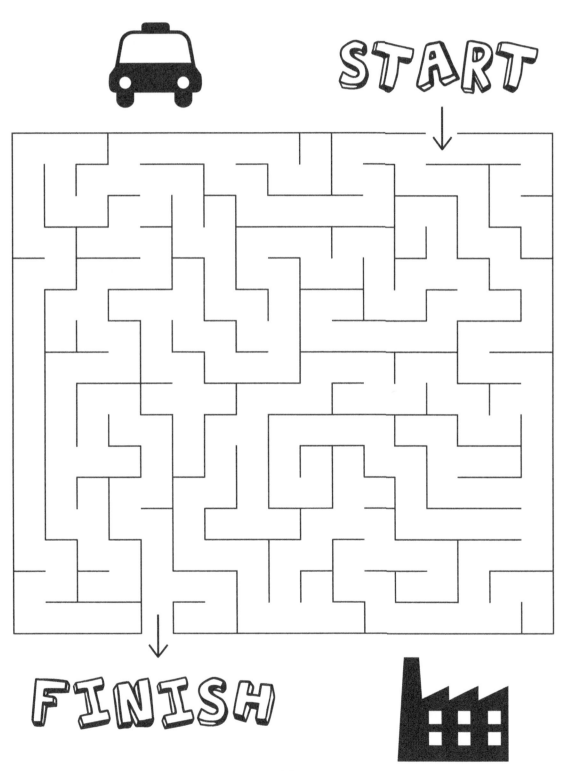

Chapter 8

Activity 6. Coloring Page

Use your imagination and color the picture.

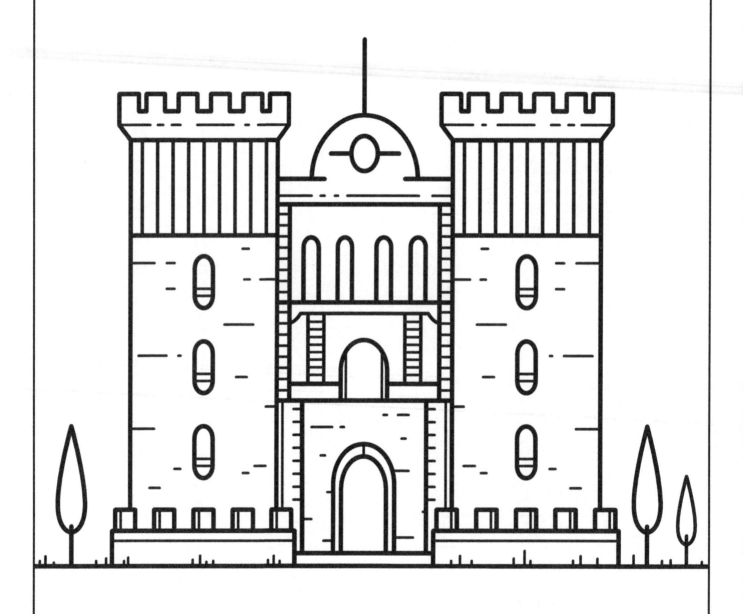

City

Activity 7. Spot the Differences

Find five differences in the second picture.

Activity 8. Math Game

The thick frame has a 3x3 grid with places for nine numbers. The squares outside of it are sums of the digits in the grid's columns, rows, and diagonals — follow the arrows.

Fill in all the blanks with whole numbers. Note that they may sometimes repeat.

			↗	
				20
7		4	→	22
		3	→	15
↓	↓	↓	↘	
20	16			17

Answers on pages 98-99   - 65 -

Chapter 8

Activity 9. Math Riddle

Solve the equation, knowing that each identical picture is assigned a specific number. If possible, try not to take any notes.

$$\text{(bus)} \times \text{(bus)} \times \text{(bus)} = 8$$

$$\text{(bank)} - \text{(bus)} = 1$$

$$\text{(church)} \div \text{(bank)} = 3$$

$$\text{(church)} \times \text{(bus)} \div \text{(bank)} = \ldots$$

Answers on page 99

Activity 10. Sudoku

There are 81 squares in a 9x9 grid in front of you. Some of them already contain numbers, and your task is to fill in the rest.

To complete it correctly, ensure that each of the nine 3x3 grids, columns, and rows contains all the digits from 1 to 9.

				5		2	1	
9		7	8	4			5	6
		2	7	3		9		4
1	2			8		7		5
		4	2		7			9
7		9	5	6	4	8	2	
			4				7	3
2			1			4		8
					3	5	9	

Congratulations!

You have just finished the eighth chapter of this book!

Chapter 9

Activity 1. Begins With

For each letter listed below, write down one word associated with flights and cruises. They can be nouns, verbs, or adjectives.

A word that begins with A is _____

A word that begins with B is _____

A word that begins with C is _____

A word that begins with D is _____

A word that begins with L is _____

A word that begins with P is _____

A word that begins with S is _____

A word that begins with T is _____

Now it's time to build and write down a meaningful sentence, including at least five of the words you wrote above.

_____

_____

_____

Flights and cruises

Activity 2. Rhyme Game

Write down two words you came up with in the previous activity; one that sounds the most positive and one the most negative. Then, find two rhyming words for each of them.

The most positive word I wrote down is _____

It rhymes with _____ and _____

The most negative word I wrote down is _____

It rhymes with _____ and _____

Activity 3. Unscrambling

Unscramble words related to flights and cruises. They can be either nouns, verbs, or adjectives. If you have difficulty with any of them, you can find all the solutions in another activity on the next page.

ODBARA - A _ _ _ _ D   GELAGUG - L _ _ _ _ _ E

ORRIATP - A _ _ _ _ _ T   TOOAMTBOR - M _ _ _ R _ _ _ T

LIESA - A _ _ _ _   ANEPRGESS - P _ _ _ E _ _ _ R

LAARVRI - A _ _ _ _ _ L   SOTPRAPS - P _ _ S _ _ _ T

RODBIAGN - B _ _ R _ _ _ G   TPLOI - P _ _ _ _

IANTPAC - C _ _ _ _ _ N   EANLP - P _ _ _ _

SUTOSCM - C _ _ _ _ _ S   SDERATW - S _ _ _ _ _ D

PRREETUAD - D _ _ _ R _ _ _ E   EASCTSIU - S _ _ _ _ _ _ E

MSDICOET - D _ _ _ S _ _ C   ETTKIC - T _ _ _ _ _

ADNGLIN - L _ _ _ _ _ G   UBERCTEULN - T _ _ B _ _ E _ _ E

Chapter 9

Activity 4. Word Search

Find and mark on the grid words, which are listed below. You can spot them horizontally or vertically – backwards and forwards.

ABOARD	CAPTAIN	LUGGAGE	PLANE
AIRPORT	CUSTOMS	MOTORBOAT	STEWARD
AISLE	DEPARTURE	PASSENGER	SUITCASE
ARRIVAL	DOMESTIC	PASSPORT	TICKET
BOARDING	LANDING	PILOT	TURBULENCE

```
M  D  P  L  A  N  E  O  F  E  W  K  J  A  X
O  O  H  P  R  P  A  S  S  E  N  G  E  R  Q
T  M  S  O  N  T  C  A  P  T  A  I  N  B  P
O  E  T  I  C  K  E  T  V  V  B  K  B  X  A
R  S  R  L  W  A  A  E  D  A  O  I  D  S  S
B  T  N  G  Q  R  R  G  R  Y  A  Z  E  M  S
O  I  N  A  R  D  R  A  A  P  R  I  P  O  P
A  C  S  I  O  T  I  G  O  I  D  D  A  T  O
T  K  U  R  G  M  V  G  B  K  I  Q  R  S  R
X  N  I  P  S  F  A  U  A  I  N  B  T  U  T
U  R  T  O  F  Z  L  L  B  N  G  R  U  C  Y
R  D  C  R  P  E  C  N  E  L  U  B  R  U  T
R  F  A  T  R  Z  T  T  O  L  I  P  E  H  P
T  V  S  A  I  S  L  E  S  T  E  W  A  R  D
S  S  E  B  X  Q  G  N  I  D  N  A  L  R  N
```

Answers on page 100

Flights and cruises

Activity 5. Maze

Find the way out going through the maze.

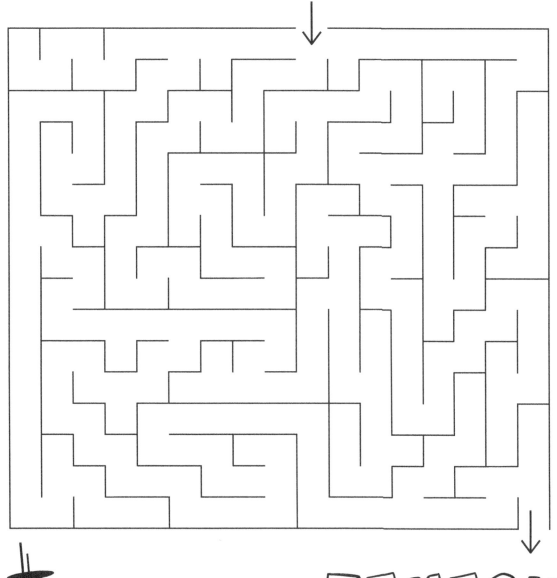

Chapter 9

Activity 6. Coloring Page

Use your imagination and color the picture.

Flights and cruises

Activity 7. Spot the Differences

Find five differences in the second picture.

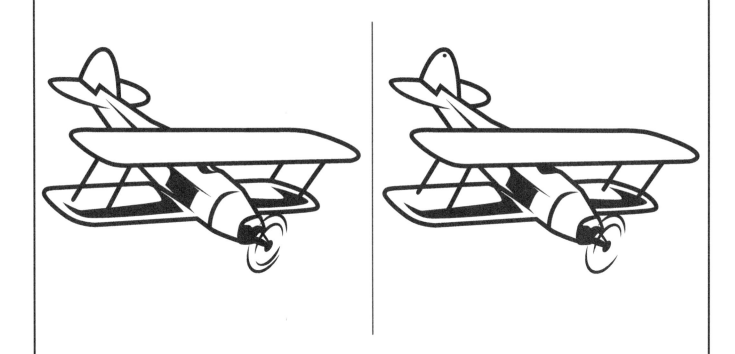

Activity 8. Math Game

The thick frame has a 3x3 grid with places for nine numbers. The squares outside of it are sums of the digits in the grid's columns, rows, and diagonals – follow the arrows.

Fill in all the blanks with whole numbers. Note that they may sometimes repeat.

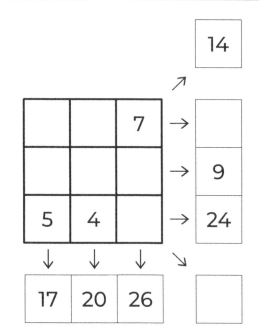

Chapter 9

Activity 9. Math Riddle

Solve the equation, knowing that each identical picture is assigned a specific number. If possible, try not to take any notes.

$$\text{✈} \times \text{✈} = 16$$

$$\text{🎈} + \text{✈} = 7$$

$$\text{⛵} - \text{🎈} = 8$$

$$\text{⛵} - \text{✈} - \text{🎈} = \ldots$$

Answers on page 101

Flights and cruises

Activity 10. Sudoku

There are 81 squares in a 9x9 grid in front of you. Some of them already contain numbers, and your task is to fill in the rest.

To complete it correctly, ensure that each of the nine 3x3 grids, columns, and rows contains all the digits from 1 to 9.

9	5	8				6		
1		3	9			8		4
			3	2	8			
5		7	1			2	8	
3		2	6	8		5	4	9
8			5				1	3
	8	4			3	9	5	
6		5				4		7
	9						6	8

Congratulations!

You have just finished the ninth chapter of this book!

Chapter 10

Activity 1. Begins With

For each letter listed below, write down one word associated with hotels and restaurants. They can be nouns, verbs, or adjectives.

A word that begins with B is _____

A word that begins with D is _____

A word that begins with H is _____

A word that begins with L is _____

A word that begins with O is _____

A word that begins with R is _____

A word that begins with S is _____

A word that begins with T is _____

Now it's time to build and write down a meaningful sentence, including at least five of the words you wrote above.

_____

_____

_____

Hotels and restaurants

Activity 2. Rhyme Game

Write down two words you came up with in the previous activity; one that sounds the most positive and one the most negative. Then, find two rhyming words for each of them.

The most positive word I wrote down is _____

It rhymes with _____ and _____

The most negative word I wrote down is _____

It rhymes with _____ and _____

Activity 3. Unscrambling

Unscramble words related to hotels and restaurants. They can be either nouns, verbs, or adjectives. If you have difficulty with any of them, you can find all the solutions in another activity on the next page.

INMTAESEI - A _ _ _ I _ _ _ S

NYCLBOA - B _ _ _ _ _ Y

TAFAERBSK - B _ _ _ K _ _ _ T

ADCLEN - C _ _ _ _ _

HKCNIEC - C _ _ _ _ _ N

EIUDSOCLI - D _ _ _ C _ _ _ S

PDEOTSI - D _ _ _ _ _ T

NRIDK - D _ _ _ _

NHUREG - H _ _ _ _ _

BOBLY - L _ _ _ _

OUXSIUURL - L _ _ _ R _ _ _ S

ERRDO - O _ _ _ _

SATPA - P _ _ _ _

ETORNIPCE - R _ _ _ P _ _ _ N

DAWSINHC - S _ _ _ _ _ _ H

SUCEA - S _ _ _ _

ESREV - S _ _ _ _

EWTOL - T _ _ _ _

NVGAE - V _ _ _ _

TWASEIRS - W _ _ _ _ _ _ S

Chapter 10

Activity 4. Word Search

Find and mark on the grid words, which are listed below. You can spot them horizontally or vertically – backwards and forwards.

AMENITIES	DELICIOUS	LUXURIOUS	SAUCE
BALCONY	DEPOSIT	ORDER	SERVE
BREAKFAST	DRINK	PASTA	TOWEL
CANDLE	HUNGER	RECEPTION	VEGAN
CHICKEN	LOBBY	SANDWICH	WAITRESS

```
A  T  S  A  P  B  T  X  P  L  K  S  X  T  L
O  R  D  E  R  R  O  V  I  D  N  E  N  B  V
S  E  X  U  M  E  W  U  L  J  E  R  V  A  A
U  G  A  K  C  A  E  D  Q  B  K  V  A  L  Z
O  N  C  N  A  K  L  S  A  U  C  E  L  C  U
I  U  A  I  N  F  U  W  I  M  I  A  T  O  M
R  H  D  R  D  A  B  K  J  T  H  D  V  N  V
U  T  R  D  L  S  Y  F  E  X  C  K  N  Y  I
X  I  P  C  E  T  D  E  L  I  C  I  O  U  S
U  S  E  A  M  E  N  I  T  I  E  S  P  B  P
L  O  R  E  C  E  P  T  I  O  N  C  J  S  Y
N  P  S  S  E  R  T  I  A  W  Q  H  N  I  X
T  E  K  V  V  R  V  V  E  G  A  N  K  R  F
R  D  K  E  X  V  H  A  V  L  O  B  B  Y  N
S  A  N  D  W  I  C  H  G  S  Y  Q  M  K  S
```

Answers on page 102

Hotels and restaurants

Activity 5. Maze

Find the way out going through the maze.

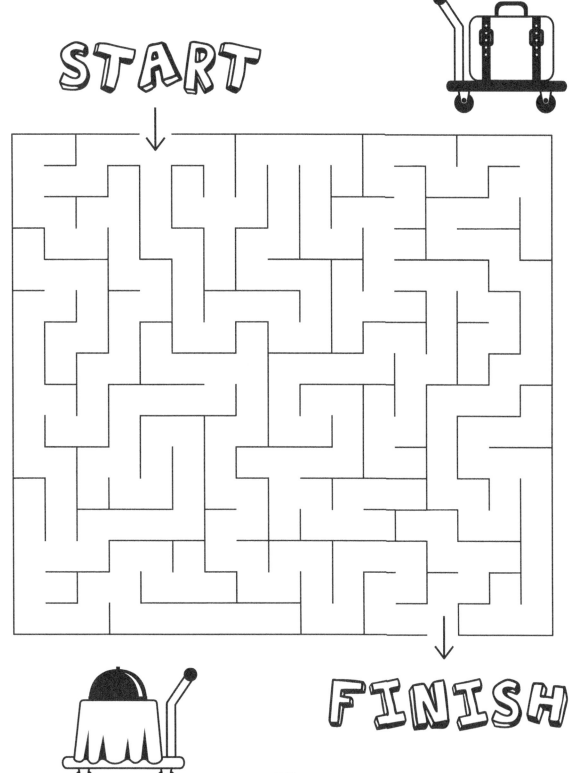

Chapter 10

Activity 6. Coloring Page

Use your imagination and color the picture.

Hotels and restaurants

Activity 7. Spot the Differences

Find five differences in the second picture.

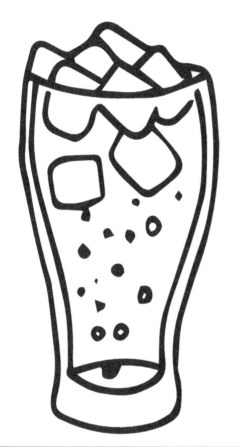
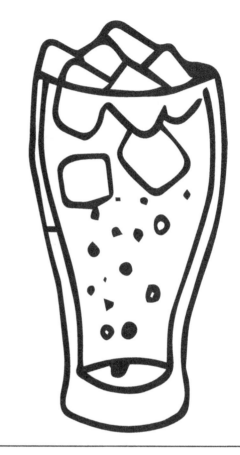

Activity 8. Math Game

The thick frame has a 3x3 grid with places for nine numbers. The squares outside of it are sums of the digits in the grid's columns, rows, and diagonals – follow the arrows.

Fill in all the blanks with whole numbers. Note that they may sometimes repeat.

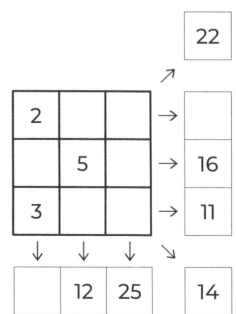

Answers on pages 102-103

Chapter 10

Activity 9. Math Riddle

Solve the equation, knowing that each identical picture is assigned a specific number. If possible, try not to take any notes.

$$\text{Key} + \text{Key} + \text{Key} = 27$$

$$\text{Key} \div \text{TV} = 3$$

$$\text{Cocktail} - \text{TV} = 1$$

$$\text{Key} - \text{TV} + \text{Cocktail} = \ldots$$

    Answers on page 103

Activity 10. Sudoku

There are 81 squares in a 9x9 grid in front of you. Some of them already contain numbers, and your task is to fill in the rest.

To complete it correctly, ensure that each of the nine 3x3 grids, columns, and rows contains all the digits from 1 to 9.

	2				5			1
	5	1		3		2	4	9
7	4	3	1	2				
2			6	5	4			
8		6		7	1		9	4
			9	8				2
	7	9		4			1	5
		4	3			9	2	
		2		9				3

Congratulations!

You have just finished the tenth chapter of this book!

Activity 4. Word Search

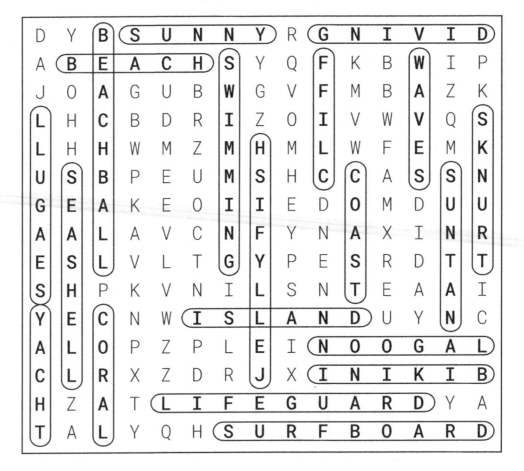

Activity 7.

Spot the Differences

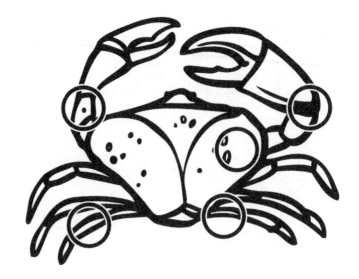

Answers - Chapter 1

Activity 8. Math Game

15		

↗

7	5	4	→	16
8	5	1	→	14
6	12	6	→	24

↓ ↓ ↓ ↘

21	22	11		18

Activity 9. Math Riddle

 = 5

 = 2

 = 6

... = 3

Activity 10. Sudoku

9	4	1	6	2	5	8	7	3
8	7	3	4	1	9	2	5	6
2	5	6	3	8	7	1	4	9
1	8	4	9	3	2	7	6	5
3	9	2	5	7	6	4	1	8
7	6	5	1	4	8	9	3	2
6	3	7	2	9	1	5	8	4
4	2	8	7	5	3	6	9	1
5	1	9	8	6	4	3	2	7

Answers - Chapter 2

Activity 4. Word Search

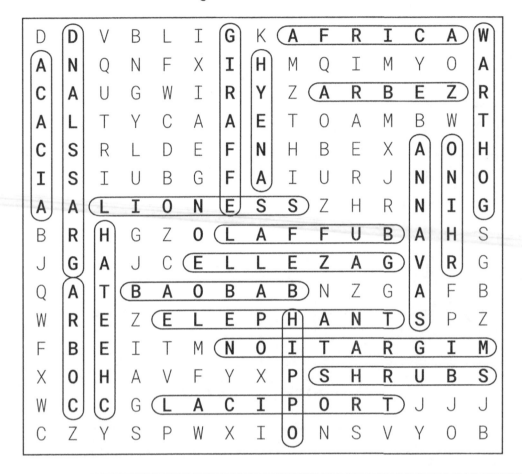

D	D	V	B	L	I	G	K	A	F	R	I	C	A	W
A	N	Q	N	F	X	I	H	M	Q	I	M	Y	O	A
C	A	U	G	W	I	R	Y	Z	A	R	B	E	Z	R
A	L	T	Y	C	A	A	E	T	O	A	M	B	W	T
I	S	R	L	D	E	F	N	H	B	E	X	A	O	H
A	S	I	U	B	G	F	A	I	U	R	J	N	N	O
A	A	L	I	O	N	E	S	S	Z	H	R	N	I	G
B	R	H	G	Z	O	L	A	F	F	U	B	A	H	S
J	G	A	J	C	E	L	L	E	Z	A	G	V	R	G
Q	A	T	E	B	A	O	B	A	B	N	Z	G	A	B
W	R	E	Z	E	L	E	P	H	A	N	T	S	P	Z
F	B	E	I	T	M	N	O	I	T	A	R	G	I	M
X	O	H	A	V	F	Y	X	P	S	H	R	U	B	S
W	C	C	G	L	A	C	I	P	O	R	T	J	J	J
C	Z	Y	S	P	W	X	I	O	N	S	V	Y	O	B

Activity 7.

Spot the Differences

Answers - Chapter 2

Activity 8. Math Game

37

↗

3	4	12	→	19
8	7	6	→	21
18	2	6	→	26

↓ ↓ ↓   ↘

29	13	24		16

Activity 9. Math Riddle

🐘 = 7

🌳 = 8

🧍 = 4

... = 11

Activity 10. Sudoku

3	6	5	8	4	9	1	7	2
1	4	2	6	3	7	5	8	9
8	7	9	5	1	2	6	4	3
2	1	3	9	7	5	4	6	8
5	9	4	1	6	8	3	2	7
7	8	6	4	2	3	9	1	5
4	5	7	2	9	6	8	3	1
9	3	1	7	8	4	2	5	6
6	2	8	3	5	1	7	9	4

Answers - Chapter 3

Activity 4. Word Search

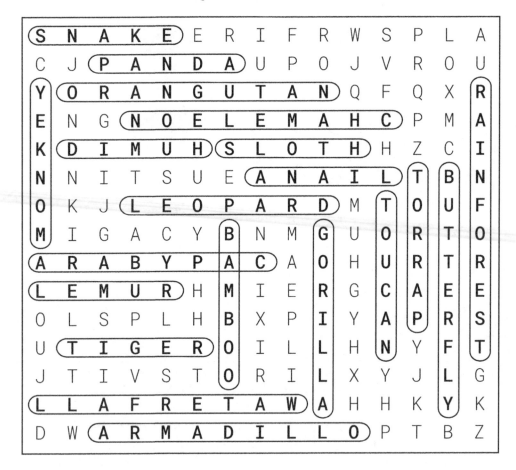

Activity 7.

Spot the Differences

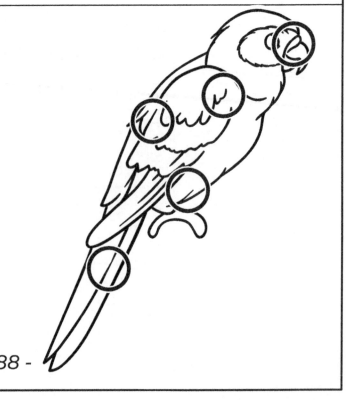

Answers - Chapter 3

Activity 8. Math Game

				15

6	4	1	→	11
2	10	8	→	20
4	12	9	→	25

↓ ↓ ↓

12	26	18		25

Activity 9. Math Riddle

 = 4

 = 6

 = 5

... = 3

Activity 10. Sudoku

3	5	4	8	7	9	2	1	6
6	8	9	3	1	2	4	5	7
2	1	7	4	6	5	8	3	9
1	7	8	9	5	6	3	2	4
9	6	3	2	8	4	1	7	5
4	2	5	1	3	7	9	6	8
8	3	6	5	9	1	7	4	2
7	9	2	6	4	3	5	8	1
5	4	1	7	2	8	6	9	3

Activity 4. Word Search

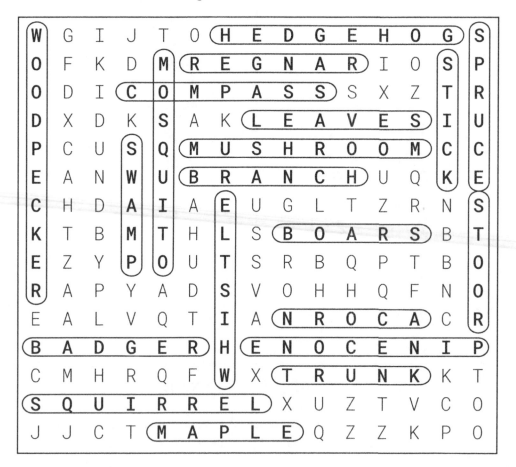

Activity 7.

Spot the Differences

Answers - Chapter 4

Activity 8. Math Game

				19

9	5	3	→	17
2	4	5	→	11
12	5	3	→	20

23	14	11		16

Activity 9. Math Riddle

 = 6

 = 4

 = 8

... = 3

Activity 10. Sudoku

4	2	6	5	1	9	7	8	3
5	9	3	7	2	8	1	6	4
7	8	1	4	6	3	5	9	2
8	7	2	1	3	5	9	4	6
9	3	4	2	7	6	8	5	1
6	1	5	9	8	4	2	3	7
2	6	9	8	4	1	3	7	5
3	5	7	6	9	2	4	1	8
1	4	8	3	5	7	6	2	9

Activity 4. Word Search

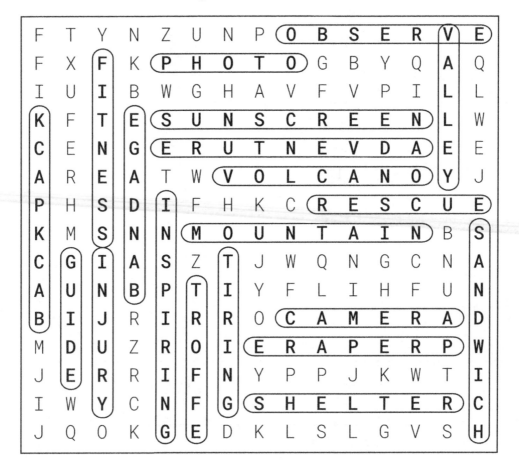

Activity 7.

Spot the Differences

Answers - Chapter 5

Activity 8. Math Game

22

↗

12	4	3	→	19
1	7	5	→	13
12	6	1	→	19

↓ ↓ ↓ ↘

25	17	9		20

Activity 9. Math Riddle

 = 7

 = 3

 = 9

... = 5

Activity 10. Sudoku

9	5	1	8	7	2	4	6	3
8	3	2	4	5	6	1	9	7
7	6	4	1	9	3	2	8	5
3	2	5	9	8	4	7	1	6
1	9	8	7	6	5	3	2	4
4	7	6	3	2	1	9	5	8
5	8	7	2	4	9	6	3	1
6	1	9	5	3	7	8	4	2
2	4	3	6	1	8	5	7	9

Answers - Chapter 6

Activity 4. Word Search

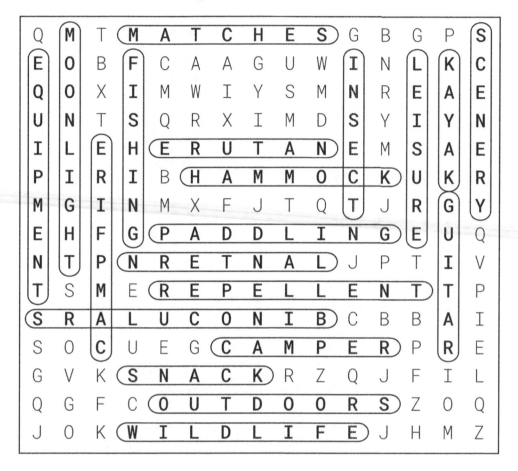

Activity 7.

Spot the Differences

Answers - Chapter 6

Activity 8. Math Game

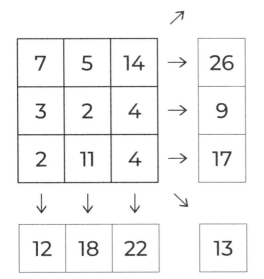

				18
7	5	14	→	26
3	2	4	→	9
2	11	4	→	17
↓	↓	↓	↘	
12	18	22		13

Activity 9. Math Riddle

 = 6

 = 4

 = 7

... = 17

Activity 10. Sudoku

1	7	5	6	2	9	8	3	4
2	4	8	1	7	3	5	9	6
6	3	9	5	8	4	2	1	7
5	2	6	8	9	7	3	4	1
3	8	7	2	4	1	9	6	5
9	1	4	3	6	5	7	8	2
7	6	3	9	1	2	4	5	8
4	5	1	7	3	8	6	2	9
8	9	2	4	5	6	1	7	3

Activity 4. Word Search

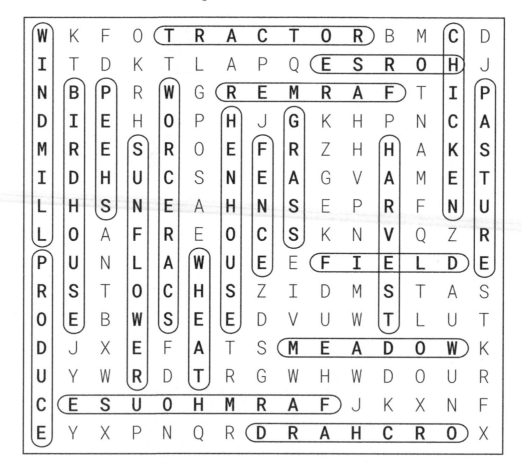

Activity 7.

Spot the Differences

Answers - Chapter 7

Activity 8. Math Game

				19

4	2	9	→	15
8	1	5	→	14
9	20	13	→	42

↓	↓	↓	
21	23	27	18

Activity 9. Math Riddle

 = 3

 = 4

 = 8

... = 9

Activity 10. Sudoku

1	8	9	3	7	4	6	2	5
3	6	5	8	9	2	7	4	1
7	2	4	1	5	6	9	3	8
6	9	7	5	1	3	4	8	2
4	5	1	2	8	9	3	6	7
8	3	2	6	4	7	5	1	9
9	7	6	4	2	1	8	5	3
2	4	8	7	3	5	1	9	6
5	1	3	9	6	8	2	7	4

Answers - Chapter 8

Activity 4. Word Search

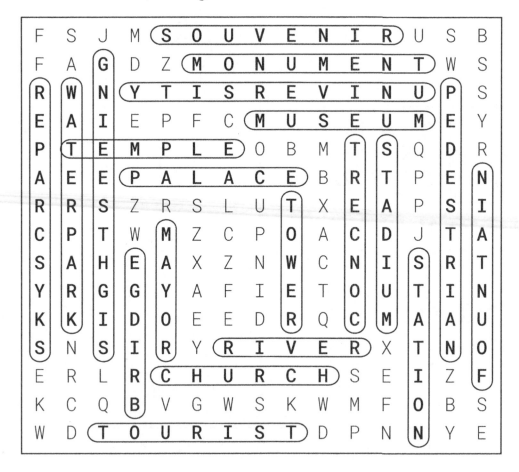

F S J M (S O U V E N I R) U S B
F A G D Z (M O N U M E N T) W S
(R) W N D (Y T I S R E V I N U) (P) S
E A N I E P F C (M U S E U M) E S
P A I (T E M P L E) O B M T S D Y
A E E (P A L A C E) B B R T E R
R R S Z R S L U T X E A S I
C P T W M Z C P O A C D T A
S A H E A X Z N W C N U R N
Y R G G Y A F I E E O U I Z
K K I D O E E D R Q C M A N
S N S R R Y (R I V E R) X (S) N Z
E R L I (C H U R C H) S E T I B
K C Q B V G W S K W M F O B
W D (T O U R I S T) D P N (N) Y

Activity 7.

Spot the Differences

Answers - Chapter 8

Activity 8. Math Game

35

↗

3	3	14	→	20
7	11	4	→	22
10	2	3	→	15

↓ ↓ ↓ ↘

20	16	21		17

Activity 9. Math Riddle

 = 2

 = 3

 = 9

... = 6

Activity 10. Sudoku

3	4	8	9	5	6	2	1	7
9	1	7	8	4	2	3	5	6
5	6	2	7	3	1	9	8	4
1	2	6	3	8	9	7	4	5
8	5	4	2	1	7	6	3	9
7	3	9	5	6	4	8	2	1
6	9	5	4	2	8	1	7	3
2	7	3	1	9	5	4	6	8
4	8	1	6	7	3	5	9	2

Answers - Chapter 9

Activity 4. Word Search

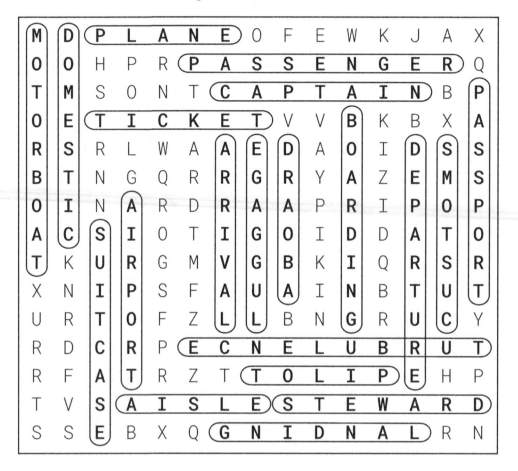

Activity 7.

Spot the Differences

Answers - Chapter 9

Activity 8. Math Game

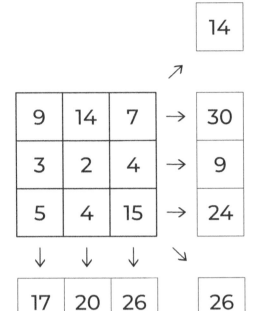

14

9	14	7	→	30
3	2	4	→	9
5	4	15	→	24

↓	↓	↓
17	20	26

26

Activity 9. Math Riddle

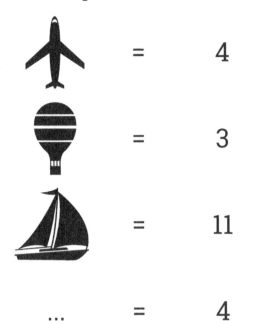

✈	=	4
🎈	=	3
⛵	=	11
...	=	4

Activity 10. Sudoku

9	5	8	7	1	4	6	3	2
1	2	3	9	5	6	8	7	4
4	7	6	3	2	8	1	9	5
5	4	7	1	3	9	2	8	6
3	1	2	6	8	7	5	4	9
8	6	9	5	4	2	7	1	3
7	8	4	2	6	3	9	5	1
6	3	5	8	9	1	4	2	7
2	9	1	4	7	5	3	6	8

Answers - Chapter 10

Activity 4. Word Search

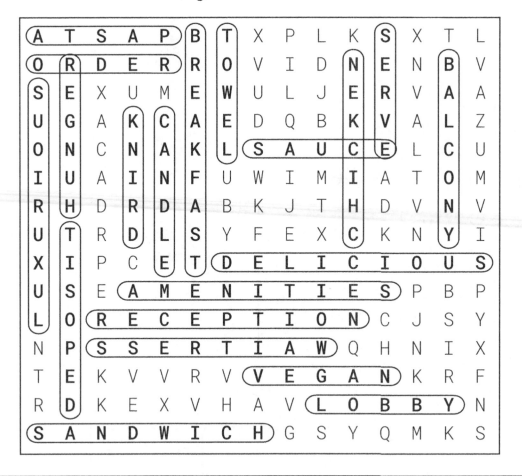

Activity 7.

Spot the Differences

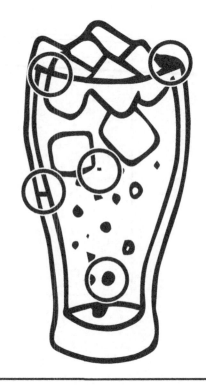

Answers - Chapter 10

Activity 8. Math Game

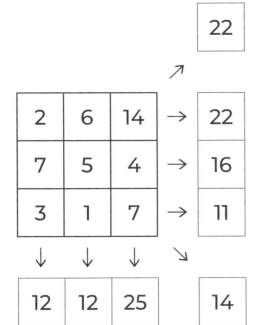

2	6	14	→	22
7	5	4	→	16
3	1	7	→	11

22

12 12 25   14

Activity 9. Math Riddle

   =   9

   =   3

   =   4

...   =   10

Activity 10. Sudoku

9	2	8	4	6	5	3	7	1
6	5	1	7	3	8	2	4	9
7	4	3	1	2	9	8	5	6
2	9	7	6	5	4	1	3	8
8	3	6	2	7	1	5	9	4
4	1	5	9	8	3	7	6	2
3	7	9	8	4	2	6	1	5
5	8	4	3	1	6	9	2	7
1	6	2	5	9	7	4	8	3

For more similar books,

visit Amazon and search for

| Loyal Sheep Publishing |

Alternatively, you can scan

the relevant QR code below.

United States   **United Kingdom**   Canada

We are delighted you made it!

We hope that our book met your expectations
and provided you moments of real joy.

We would greatly appreciate it if you could leave
a review of this book (e.g., using the QR code below)
or recommend it to someone you know would love it.

United States

United Kingdom

Canada

That would be a massive help in making
this book available to more people
who may benefit from such activities!

Thank you a lot and see you soon!

Printed in Great Britain
by Amazon

24608020R00059